Blue Sky Bluebird

Rick Chrustowski

Henry Holt and Company
New York

Henry Holt and Company, LLC
Publishers since 1866
115 West 18th Street
New York, New York 10011
www.henryholt.com

Henry Holt is a registered trademark of Henry Holt and Company, LLC
Copyright © 2004 by Rick Chrustowski
All rights reserved.
Distributed in Canada by H. B. Fenn and Company Ltd.

Library of Congress Cataloging-in-Publication Data
Chrustowski, Rick.
Blue sky bluebird / Rick Chrustowski.
Summary: Follows a family of bluebirds from the completion of a nest at the beginning
of spring through the migration of the parents and eight fledglings in autumn.
1. Bluebirds—Juvenile literature. [1. Bluebirds. 2. Birds.] I. Title.
QL696.P288C49 2004   598.8′42—dc21   2003006874

ISBN 0-8050-7104-0 / First Edition—2004 / Designed by Amy Manzo Toth
Printed in the United States of America on acid-free paper. ∞

10 9 8 7 6 5 4 3 2 1

The artist used up to forty layers of colored pencil over watercolor wash on
140-pound watercolor paper to create the illustrations for this book.

For my sisters: Jan, Mary Ellen, Lynn, and Amy
—R. C.

One spring day, when the ground is a carpet of green, a pair of bluebirds arrive at their summer home. After they mate, the female weaves layers of coarse grass into a circle inside their nest box. Then she presses her body into the middle to make a cup. An egg forms inside her body as she works. Just before it is laid, the egg turns as blue as a summer sky.

Each morning at dawn, the female lays a new egg until there are four in her clutch. She stays on her nest for the next two weeks, leaving only for short trips to get water and stretch her wings.

Nestled under the female's warm belly, tiny chicks begin to grow inside the eggs.

Peek Inside an Egg

The egg starts when a yolk sac forms inside the mother's body. The embryo, or developing chick, first appears as a small white bump on the yolk. The yolk is wrapped in egg white, and finally a shell is formed.

Once the egg is laid, the yolk feeds the growing embryo through a web of blood vessels. After five days, the embryo begins to look like a little bird. It has eyes and a beak, stubby wings, and long toes.

After fourteen days, the egg is a tight fit. The chick pokes its beak into a small chamber of air at one end of the egg and breathes for the first time. Now it is ready to hatch.

Early one morning at the end of May, three bluebird chicks break out of their shells. The fourth egg is silent. The mother bluebird leans close to listen.

Tap. Tap. Pip. Peep! A chick is hard at work inside. He pecks a line of holes around the top of his shell with a special egg tooth at the tip of his beak. Then he s-t-r-e-t-c-h-e-s out and pushes his shell open.

Naked and helpless, the last baby bluebird flops into the nest. Now he is called a nestling. Soon his egg tooth drops off, and tufts of gray fuzz appear on his head and back. In a few hours, he lifts his wobbly head and joins his sisters as they beg for food.

Ten days later, the mother and father birds rush food to their young every few minutes from sunup to sundown. Plump caterpillars, leggy spiders, and crunchy grasshoppers disappear in seconds down the chicks' gaping gullets.

Between feedings the nestlings flap their newly feathered wings or nap in a heap for extra warmth. Sometimes the females use their little brother as a step stool to get a better view.

When the nestlings are nineteen days old, they take turns peeking out of the entrance hole. They are fully grown now, and the nest is crowded. The mother and father bring in less food. Instead, they dangle insects from their beaks to lure the chicks out of the nest.

The oldest chick takes the bait first. She hurries to the entrance hole, hops forward, and out she goes, into the world! Twenty minutes later, the other two females hop out one after the other. The last chick, the little male with blue wings, refuses to leave.

His mother pokes her head in and tries to coax him out
with a shiny cricket. His father brings him a fat beetle grub.
The chick doesn't budge.
Hungry and shivering, the bluebird ruffles his feathers like
a blanket and sleeps the long night alone in the nest box.

When morning comes, the steady thrum of insects fades away. The bluebird hears his parents sing outside. He scrambles to the opening and leans forward—farther . . . farther . . . he's out! Wings flapping wildly, the bluebird launches into the air. He is a fledgling at last.

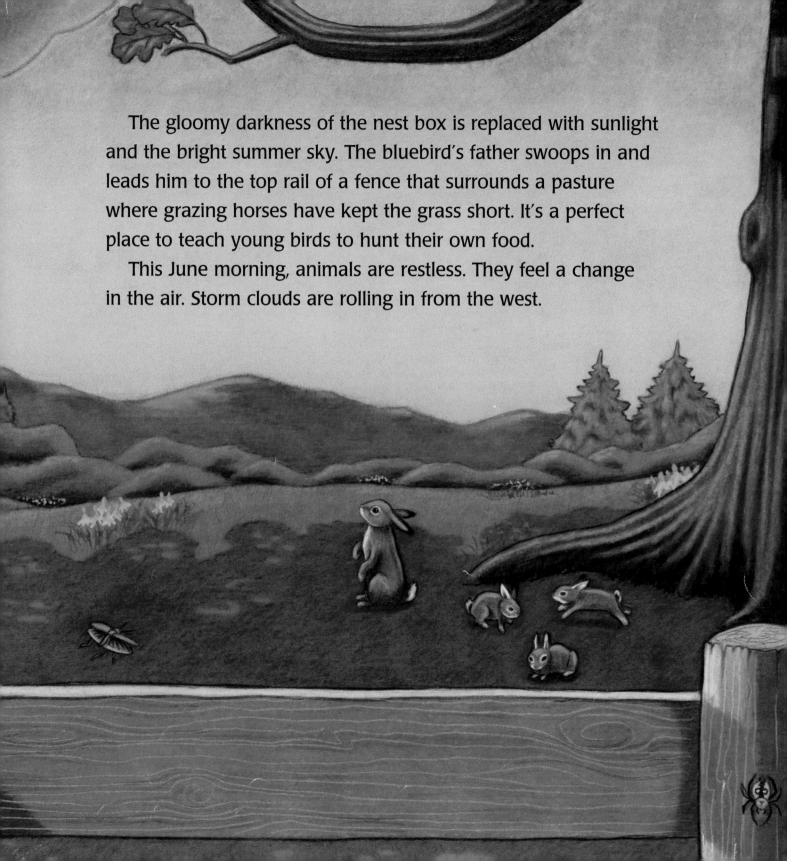

The gloomy darkness of the nest box is replaced with sunlight and the bright summer sky. The bluebird's father swoops in and leads him to the top rail of a fence that surrounds a pasture where grazing horses have kept the grass short. It's a perfect place to teach young birds to hunt their own food.

This June morning, animals are restless. They feel a change in the air. Storm clouds are rolling in from the west.

The mother and father bluebirds gather their fledglings in a tree. As the wind shifts direction, heated air pushes clouds higher into the sky. This updraft feeds the clouds, which become giant thunderheads.

By late afternoon, raindrops splatter down. The parent bluebirds warble softly to reassure their young.

Raindrops become a pelting downpour as the storm erupts. Suddenly a blinding flash of light streaks across the sky. *Kaaa Booooom!* A crack of thunder rattles the ground. The bluebirds scatter like leaves in the wind.

Then, as quickly as it started, the storm is over. Sunlight streams through breaks in the clouds. The last heavy raindrops splash to the ground.

The bluebirds search for their fledglings. One female is hiding in a cedar tree. Another ducked into a shrub. Another found a tree hole.

But the male is missing. His parents call for him. Finally they see him, feathers soaked, clinging to the spot where he was before the storm.

For the next few weeks, the bluebird and his sisters follow their father. He shows them how to hunt insects by choosing a low perch and then pouncing down to the ground.

Once the fledglings can gather food on their own, the parents renew their mating bond. The male flutters his wings like a butterfly, fans his tail, and sings to his mate. The female wing-waves and warbles a song of her own.

She builds a new nest. Then, perfectly timed with the great supply of insects in late summer, she lays a second clutch of eggs.

In August after the new chicks hatch, the young bluebird and his sisters help their parents raise the second brood. They practice flying and landing as they chase insects to feed their younger siblings. The whole family work together as a team, feeding the young and watching for predators. Summer lasts just long enough for the new chicks to leave the nest.

The bluebird and his siblings lose their juvenile feathers and grow adult plumage by early fall. After a cold snap cuts down the number of insects, the family begin to fly south to their wintering grounds. Along the way, they stop to fuel up on wild grapes and sumac berries.

Soon the fresh growth of spring will call them northward again, and the bluebirds will go their separate ways. Then the young male bluebird will return to the countryside where he was born to look for a mate and a nest box where he can raise a family of his own.

Bluebird News

Eastern Bluebird

Western Bluebird

Bluebirds live in cities and suburbs, but they love the open fields of farm country. The best place to see them is perched on telephone wires or fences along rural roads.

Not long ago, bluebirds were hard to find. Their habitat is steadily being replaced by housing developments and strip malls. Invasive birds like starlings and European house sparrows compete with them for nesting cavities in trees.

Bird lovers across America are putting up nest boxes made especially for blue-birds. Some people monitor long rows, or "bluebird trails," of nest boxes in prime habitats. Over the years, thousands of young bluebirds have fledged from these boxes, and now the news is good—bluebirds are making a comeback.

Bluebirds are agile songbirds that belong to the thrush family. Like their cousin, the robin, bluebird young have spotted breasts. Bluebirds that escape the watchful eyes of hawks, snakes, and raccoons can live to be five years old.

Bluebirds can be found throughout the United States into Canada and Mexico. There are three different kinds of bluebird. All females look similar: They are brownish-gray, with blue on their wings and tail. The males are distinctly different shades of blue. Eastern bluebirds, like the one in this book, are cobalt blue and live in the eastern part of North America, from the Rocky Mountains east to the Atlantic Ocean. Western bluebirds are a deep purplish-blue and live in western North America, from the Rocky Mountains west to the Pacific. The largest bluebirds, mountain bluebirds, are sky blue all over. They live in the mountains and higher elevations of western North America.

Mountain Bluebird